The LITTLE INSTRUCTION BOOK for grandparents

Kate Freeman

summersdale

THE LITTLE INSTRUCTION BOOK FOR GRANDPARENTS

With research by Anna Martin

Illustrations by Kostiantyn Fedorov

Disclaimer
The advice in this book is purely for the purpose of entertainment and should not be followed.

Summersdale Publishers Ltd
46 West Street
Chichester
West Sussex
PO19 1RP
UK

www.summersdale.com

Printed and bound in the Czech Republic

ISBN: 978-1-84953-631-8

Substantial discounts on bulk quantities of Summersdale books are available to corporations, professional associations and other organisations. For details contact Nicky Douglas by telephone: +44 (0) 1243 756902, fax: +44 (0) 1243 786300 or email: nicky@summersdale.com.

To...... proud grandparents Barb & Allen

From...... co grandparents John & Trixie!

X. ♡ x.

If I had known how wonderful it would be to have grandchildren, I'd have had them first.

Lois Wyse

Ah, the joys of being a grandparent! You know already that your rose-tinted dreams of growing old gracefully and spending quality time in a comfy chair by the fire are history now, because all your spare hours are devoted to a small, slightly sticky person, who is too irresistible – and just too damn noisy – to ignore. But who is going to teach you how to operate the over-complicated travel system, or help solve that perennial problem of how to change a loaded nappy with just one wet wipe? Because let's be honest, things ain't what they used to be.

Don't worry, though! Help is at hand in the form of this little instruction book, which will guide you safely through the pitfalls and pleasures of being a grandparent, and most importantly teach you how to keep up with the little blighters. Enjoy!

How to get out of babysitting duties:

 **Feign illness.**

 **Switch the phone off, draw the curtains and stay very quiet.**

 **Emigrate.**

Granny's knitted jumpers are a Christmas staple – the brasher the better. Don't disappoint them with something shop-bought. You know they love it because they always wear it when you visit.

Bear in mind that your grandchild's favourite game is 'What's in Granny's bag?'

Downsize so your grandchildren can't sleep over.

Accept that soon you'll forget your own name and will only answer to 'Grandma' or 'Grandpa'.

Always call your grandchildren 'dear' or 'love' – it's so much easier than trying to remember all their names.

Make up outrageous stories about your past.

It seems a long way down to the floor these days – combat this by getting your grandchild to play in your raised flower beds instead. Weeding is a fun game for kids of all ages!

Threaten to take out your false teeth if they don't behave.

Insist on holding your grandchild's hand in public, no matter how old they are.

Teach them to knit or crochet – it'll keep them out of mischief when you're watching the soaps.

If you have several grandchildren to look after at once, tie a balloon to their wrists so you can spot them at a distance.

Get the photo albums out and show them all the least flattering pictures of their parents.

Grandchildren will see you as their sweetie provider for years to come – don't disappoint them.

Kick their ass on the Xbox – they will be forever in awe of you.

If you receive a sales call that you'd rather not take, hand the phone to your grandchild and get them to babble at the caller.

Always bring a book with you if you're taking your grandchild out to lunch. If they're really naughty or noisy, you can pretend you're not with them.

Get your grandchildren to eat their greens – bogies are optional.

Remember that biscuits are acceptable for breakfast, with a nice cup of tea.

Attach a baby-on-board sticker to your mobility scooter, if you have one.

Your new role models will be:

 Mary Poppins – on a good day.

 Nanny McPhee – on a bad day.

 The Terminator – on a particularly bad day.

If your grandchildren don't eat their breakfast, place the leftovers in between a couple of slices of bread and give it to them for lunch.

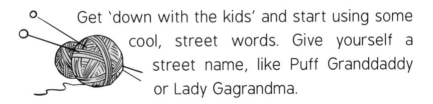

Get 'down with the kids' and start using some cool, street words. Give yourself a street name, like Puff Granddaddy or Lady Gagrandma.

Rivalry between grandparents is healthy, and a bit of competition is good for you. Try these tips to stay on top of your game:

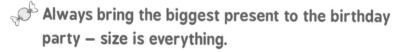 **Always bring the biggest present to the birthday party – size is everything.**

Get the first steps on the camcorder first – you can boast about it for years.

Be the first to arrive on Christmas morning – in Mr and Mrs Santa outfits.

Grandchildren have a knack for finding the most dangerous items in the house, as well as your secret chocolate stash.

Don't forget that a baby's reach is similar to that of an orangutan – move or hide anything of value.

Your new best friends will be:

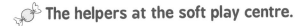 **The helpers at the soft play centre.**

The sweetshop owner.

The park keeper.

Your grandchild will be born computer literate, which means free tech support for life!

Don't bother calling your grandchild when dinner is ready; send them a text.

Remember: if your grandchild has developed bad habits, it won't be from your side of the family.

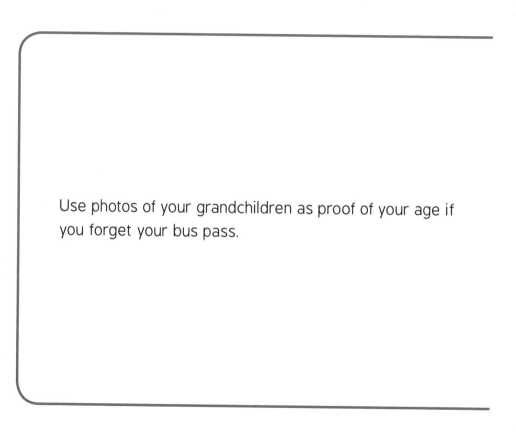

Use photos of your grandchildren as proof of your age if you forget your bus pass.

Insist on playing on all the apparatus in the play park, while your adoring grandchild watches from the comfort of their buggy – it's educational.

If your grandchild asks where your wrinkles are from, say you spent too long in the bath.

Always pick the noisiest places to eat, to drown out your grandchild's tantrums.

Insist you're snowed in and can't make it for Christmas. It'll be a whole lot cheaper, and quieter.

If you can't be a shining example to your grandchildren, be a terrible warning.

Lovely gifts to expect from your grandchildren:

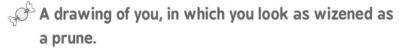 **A drawing of you, in which you look as wizened as a prune.**

A piece of misshapen pottery, with no discernible use.

School photographs, to clutter every available surface.

Use the grandchildren as spies to find out what Mum and Dad are buying you for Christmas..

Purchase matching walking frames for you and your soon-to-be-toddling grandchild.

Pretend to be asleep when your grandchild asks you to help with their homework.

Be wary of compliments from your children;
it means they're about to ask you to babysit.

If your grandchild is having
a tantrum, join in!

Let your grandchild eat off the table – they prefer it and it saves on washing up.

If you're doing babysitting duties with your partner, remember it's always their turn to change the nappy.

Blame your farts on the baby.

If your grandchildren play up while you're out, say loudly to passers-by, 'I blame the parents!'

Always be gracious when receiving a handmade present from your grandchild, no matter how disastrous.

If you're babysitting for the evening and would rather not be asked to do it on a regular basis, ring up your son/daughter and ask them to remind you how many children you should be looking after.

Make weightlifter grunts every time you pick up your grandchild.

When you find yourself scratching your head, it won't be because you're trying to remember something – even the loveliest children are not immune to nits.

Things you're likely to learn as a grandparent:

 All the names of the Octonauts and the cast of *Balamory*.

How it feels to be liked on Facebook.

That things aren't what they used to be.

Insist that there is an age limit to entering theme parks and that you surpassed it some time ago.

When meeting your grandchild for the first time, try not to say to the parents, 'One is easy, just you wait until the next one comes along.'

Indulge the little ones with sugary snacks, ideally half an hour before returning them to their parents.

Be prepared to be treated like a human climbing frame. Better still, wear a string vest to give the little ones a better footing.

Do your weekly shop with the grandchildren – that way you can use the special parent-and-child parking spaces.

When your grandchildren are at your house, be sure to follow them around with a dustpan and brush at all times.

Children grow up too fast these days – continue to buy dolls and teddies for your grandchildren no matter how old they are.

Let them eat mud – it didn't do your children any harm.

Be prepared to be asked: 'How old are you?' and 'Will you die soon?' on a regular basis.

Grandparent essentials:

🍬 **Annual passes to all the local attractions.**

🍬 **A comfy knee.**

🍬 **Sturdy shoes and all-weather gear.**

Now's the time to get the old toys and little outfits out of the loft – they're the height of vintage cool now.

 When verbalising what you really think of your son/daughter-in-law, make sure it's not in the room with the baby monitor switched on.

Pretend not to hear when they're asking for something in the toyshop – the old 'my hearing aid's playing up' trick works every time.

Teach them to tidy up after themselves – bribery helps.

Don't be surprised to find tiny tooth marks appearing on your furniture and fingerprints all over the TV.

If they won't wash their face, spit on a tissue and wipe it for them — they won't make that mistake again!

How to reprimand naughty grandchildren:

🍬 **Works for toddlers: threaten to cancel the park visit today.**

🍬 **Works for youngsters: threaten to tell Santa how naughty they've been.**

🍬 **Works on teenagers and beyond: threaten to cut them out of your will.**

Get used to hurdling the stairgate – it's great for keeping fit and flexible.

Now that you're looking after the grandchildren on a regular basis, you will find yourself spending more time at local attractions than in your own home.

Wear stain-resistant clothing at all times.

Things that will boggle your mind:

🍬 **The travel system, or what you would have known as a 'pram'.**

🍬 **Baby-signing.**

🍬 **Baby webcam monitors.**

Naptime (theirs, not yours) is the Holy Grail when looking after your grandchild for the day. Get in the habit of offering to babysit at this time.

Don't get lured into playing Twister unless you have your chiropractor on speed dial.

Enjoy those early years – the ones when they can't answer back.

Teach them how to do knots so they can tie your shoelaces – remember, your back isn't what it used to be.

Remember: there's only one thing scarier than your child borrowing your car – your grandchild borrowing it.

Combine your daily walk with
the baby with a paper round
and make a bit of money.

Ways to entertain the grandchildren on a rainy day:

🍬 Play hide and seek, and use the 'seeking' time to snatch forty winks.

🍬 Let them out into the garden with wet-weather gear and watch them from the comfort of your armchair.

🍬 Watch repeats of *Miss Marple* and explain that the children's channel doesn't work when it's raining.

Your perfectly coiffed 'do' will soon look like a small child has been styling it.

Keep a mental note of where all the baby-changing facilities are in town.

Always buy the noisiest presents and make sure any outfits are dry-clean only – not only will the grandchildren love them more, but the irritation it causes the parents is character building.

Don't worry about your grandchildren making a mess in their house – their parents can clear it up when they get home.

See your grandchildren's constant questioning as a way to keep those little grey cells in optimum condition.

Never leave any circular, flat objects, such as biscuits, near the DVD player.

It's important to learn your grandchild's cues for needing the toilet when they are potty training – either that, or insist the parents pay for carpet-cleaning services.

Remember, your grandchild will never say the new words you've just taught them when other people are around.

If you give money as a gift, they will remember the amount and expect more next birthday.

What to buy your grandchild for their first birthday:

 A lovely big cardboard box – hours of fun for a baby.

A noisy electronic toy – hours of fun for Dad.

A make-and-do kit – hours of cleaning up for Mum.

Don't be surprised to find small toys in your shoes as you try to put them on.

If your grandchildren buy you a box of chocolates, it means they expect you to share them.

Try not to show your disappointment that your children haven't named your grandchild after you, but launch into a fabulous story about the questionable origins of the unusual name they chose instead when prompted.

Don't send a self-addressed envelope for a thank-you note with your gifts, however tempting.

It's important to have a life outside of grandparent duties – but don't let them find out.

Wear glasses at all times – little ones love poking their fingers in exposed eyes.

Keep your make-up bag out of sight, unless you want the contents smeared on your grandchild and every available surface.

Take your grandchildren with you to bingo – insist it will help them learn their numbers, when really it means you have more chances of winning.

How to behave at the school play:

- Clap loudly and enthusiastically at the sight of your darling grandchild.

- Unfurl a banner to show your support.

- Use the 'hard of hearing' excuse so you get a seat at the front.

Keep your mobile phone handy at all times, just in case you get stuck in the pirate's ship in the park.

Possible responses when your grandchildren ask what their parents were like at their age:

 'Simply awful, but you won't end up like that.'

 'To be honest I think my child was switched at birth.'

 Show, don't tell — get the photo albums out so they can see for themselves.

Never say you could do with a break when you drop back the grandchildren – you might be invited on the next family holiday.

Learn all of the latest chart tunes with the help of your grandchildren – it will come in handy at the next karaoke night.

You will soon know every character by name on all the children's programmes.

Keep pets away from your grandchildren – Tiddles will thank you for it.

Essential grandparent skills:

 **Issuing toffees and sweets at regular intervals.**

 **A repertoire of magic tricks, such as producing a coin from behind an ear – better still, a fiver.**

 **Falling asleep after a big meal.**

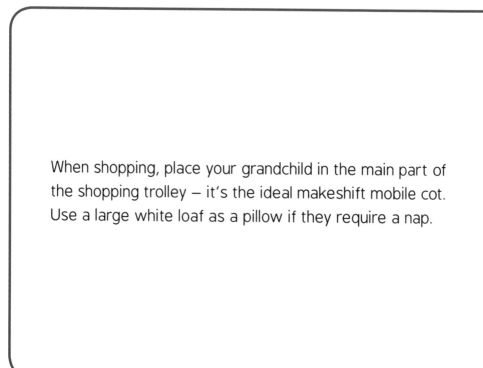

When shopping, place your grandchild in the main part of the shopping trolley – it's the ideal makeshift mobile cot. Use a large white loaf as a pillow if they require a nap.

Get used to muddy tyre tracks up and down your hall from the buggy.

Don't be surprised if the things that your grandchildren are most fascinated by are your varicose veins and crow's feet.

Don't leave any jugs, bowls or other receptacles that could be confused with a toilet in the bathroom.

Having a grandchild is a great excuse for investing in bath toys.

Grandparents are as magical as the tooth fairy and Father Christmas – take a leaf out of their books and visit either once a year, or in extreme circumstances.

Silence will be a thing of the past, unless you deliberately forget to put your hearing aid in.

Make your house a pen- and paint-free zone, at least until they're 18.

Padlock your biscuit tin.

Always take your walking stick with you when out with the grandchildren; the crook is very handy for scooping them out of the ball pool or sandpit.

If your grandchildren ask something particularly tricky, tell them to ask their parents.

Cunning ways your children will suggest that you would love to do more babysitting:

🍬 'The children are always asking when they will see you next.'

🍬 'You must get bored sitting at home.'

🍬 'They're sleeping through now, so it'll be like they're not even there.'

When they're big enough, take your grandchildren to the cinema – that way you can have a nap in a warm, dark place while they're entertained.

You won't have time for your friends any more – unless they're looking after their grandchildren too.

Take delight in the fact that your grandchildren have never heard your corny jokes before.

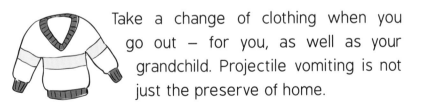

Take a change of clothing when you go out – for you, as well as your grandchild. Projectile vomiting is not just the preserve of home.

Your grandchildren will grow up fast, so capture those special moments on camera – even if they are gurning or squinting in every picture.

You will need a diary just for grandparent duties – not just for all the childcare you will be doing, but the school plays and parties.

Purchase toy versions of cooking and cleaning apparatus for your grandchild's birthdays and Christmases, then once they have become adept at using them, invite them over to your place once a week to use the real thing!

Rhyming games can be a great way to learn new words, especially expletives.

If you're feeling cold, put an extra cardigan on your grandchild.

Highlights of being a grandparent:

 **Experiencing life through a child's eyes once more.**

 **All the fun of having children, minus the sleepless nights and homework assignments.**

 **Being adored by little ones, who wouldn't dream of answering back.**

If you're after that shabby chic look in your house, invite the grandchildren round and get them to bash your furniture with strategically placed implements.

If you're interested in finding out more about our
books, find us on Facebook at **Summersdale Publishers**
and follow us on Twitter at **@Summersdale**.

www.summersdale.com